AUTHOR:

PEDRO ANDRADE

TITLE:

AUSTERITY (HI)STORY
THROUGH
SOCIOLOGICAL COMICS

SUB-TITLE:

A GUIDE TO SOCIAL MEDIA AND NETWORKS
AGAINST AUSTERITOCRACY
FOR USE BY ALL GENERATIONS

PUBLISHER/DATE:

© COMMUNICATION
AND SOCIETY RESEARCH
CENTRE,
INSTITUTE OF SOCIAL
SCIENCES, UNIVERSITY
OF MINHO,
2015

SERIES:

SOCIOLOGICAL
COMICS

ISBN:
978-1522934554

TABLE OF CONTENTS

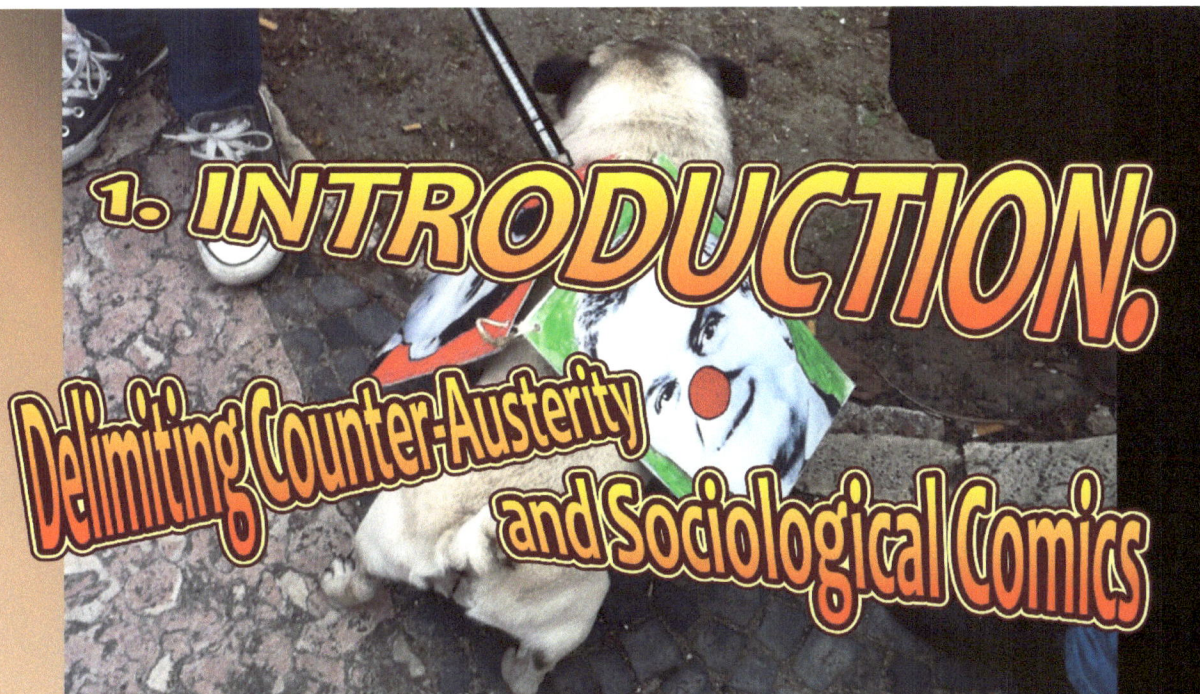

1. INTRODUCTION:
Delimiting Counter-Austerity and Sociological Comics

SOCIOLOGICAL COMICS

THIS BOOK WAS WRITTEN IN 2013 DURING THE SOCIAL EVENTS IT REPORTS, AND WAS SELECTED TO BE SHOWN AT THE 2ND EXHIBITION *OFF THE S(H)ELF': THE SELF AND SUBJECTIVITY IN THE ARTIST'S BOOK*, THAT TOOK PLACE THE 29 MAY 2015 AT I-KLECTIC ART LAB, LONDON.

THE BOOK ARTICULATES AND FUSIONS SOCIOLOGY AND DIGITAL COMICS.

THEREFORE, CONSIDERING A *STRUCTURAL AND METHODOLOGICAL POINT OF VIEW*, SUCH BOOK ESSAYS AN EXPERIMENTAL MODE OF CONTENT PRESENTATION, A GENRE NAMED *SOCIOLOGICAL COMICS*.

THIS MEANS ESSENTIALLY A SOCIOLOGICAL METHOD OF DISCUSSING *SOCIAL QUESTIONS* AND WRITING *HYPOTHESES*, THAT USES TEXT AND IMAGES INSIDE COMIC FRAMES.

WRITTEN COMICS ('BANDA ESCRITA')

IN THE GENEALOGY OF POLITICAL / CULTURAL EXPERIMENTALISM, SITUATIONIST MOVEMENT APPLIED COMICS TO CRITICIZE THE *SOCIETY OF SPECTACLE*.

IN THE LAST DECADE OF XX CENTURY, A 'WRITTEN COMICS' ('BANDA ESCRITA') EXPERIENCE WAS CARRIED OUT, EMPLOYING COMICS FRAMES THAT INCLUDED JUST TEXT AND NO IMAGES (SEE IMAGE ON THE RIGHT, PUBLISHED IN ANDRADE 1997, AND BIBLIOGRAPHY)

AIMS

CONSIDERING NOW A SUBSTANTIVE PERSPECTIVE, THIS BOOK AIMS TO ANALYZE *DISCOURSES* AND *COUNTER-DISCOURSES* ARTICULATED WITH BOTH *GLOBAL AND LOCAL PUBLIC OPINION*.

THESE ARE PARTLY ENGENDERED INSIDE THE *DIALOGIC PUBLIC SPHERE*, LIKE THE CITY SPACE, MASS MEDIA AND DIGITAL SOCIAL NETWORKS.

A CASE STUDY ON COUNTER-AUSTERITY

A CASE STUDY WAS SELECTED, ON THE *URBAN AND MEDIA STRUGGLES* OCCURRED IN 2013 IN PORTUGAL.

SUCH PROCESS DEFINED A *COUNTER-AUSTERIY STRATEGY* AGAINST THE *AUSTERITY* MEASURES IMPLEMENTED BY PORTUGUESE GOVERNMENT TO DEAL WITH THE PRESENT EUROPEAN CRISIS.

1.1. CONCEPTUAL ABSTRACT

THIS IS A CONCEPTUAL ABSTRACT

REGARDING THE MEDIUM 'BOOK', THIS INTRODUCTION INCLUDES A TOOL I NAMED 'CONCEPTUAL ABSTRACT'

THIS IS NOT A GLOSSARY

A GLOSSARY LISTS CONCEPTS AND THEIR DEFINITIONS IN A ALPHABETIC ORDER, USUALLY AFTER A TEXT.

ARGUMENTATIVE ORDER

DIFFERENTLY, A **CONCEPTUAL ABSTRACT** PRESENTS, IN THE BEGINNING OF A TEXT, THE MAIN CONCEPTS INCLUDED IN THAT TEXT, AND THEIR DEFINITIONS, WITHIN THE ORDER OF THE ARGUMENTS NECESSARY FOR A SOCIAL PROCESS' DISCUSSION.

A CONCEPTUAL STORY

SUCH DEBATE IS OFTEN BASED ON MULTIPLE **SOCIAL STORIES** TOLD BY COMMON CITIZENS AND BY SOCIAL SCIENTISTS.

WITHIN THIS PERSPECTIVE, THE CONCEPTUAL ABSTRACT WORKS AS A SORT OF **CONCEPTUAL STORY.**

OPINION TYPES

NOW, RETURNING TO THIS BOOK CONTENT:

THE MANIFESTATIONS OF **LOCAL AND SEMI-LOCAL PUBLIC OPINION** HERE PRESENTED ARE CONNECTED WITH **GLOBAL PUBLIC OPINION.**

ACCOUNTABILITY

OPINION USES ETHICAL AND AESTHETICAL **ACCOUNTABILITY STRATEGIES**, SOMETIMES INNOVATIVE, FOR COMMUNICATION AND CRITIQUE INSIDE BOTH THE URBAN PUBLIC SPHERE AND THE VIRTUAL PUBLIC SPHERE.

SOCIAL DISCONTINUITIES

WITHIN A **SUBSTANTIVE AND CONCEPTUAL PERSPECTIVE**, THIS BOOK DEPICTS A SOCIAL PROCESS WHOSE SUBJECT PERTAINS TO **SOCIAL DISCONTINUITIES AND POLITICAL RUPTURES**, STUDIED THROUGH THEIR INSTITUTIONAL AND CITIZEN ACCOUNTING.

SUCH PROCESSES OCCUR OFTEN WITHIN URBAN SPACES AND SOMETIMES INSIDE ARTISTIC SCAPES (SEE BIBLIOGRAPHY: ANDRADE ET AL, 2010)

AUSTERITY POLICIES AND POLITICS

AUSTERITOCRACY HAS BEEN DEFINED AS AN ECONOMIC, POLITICAL AND CULTURAL PERVERSION OF DEMOCRACY, A PROCESS WHERE HEGEMONIC AND SOMEHOW DICTATORIAL RULES ARE DEMOCRATICALLY DISSEMINATED FROM A CENTRAL COUNTRY OR A POLITICAL / BUROCRATIC AXIS TO ARTIFICIALLY IMPOVERISHED NATIONS WITHIN WIDE POLITICAL WEBS.

IN FACT, IN EUROPE ALONG THE LAST YEARS, AUSTERITY MEASURES PRODUCED A 'ZOMBIE ECONOMY' SUBSTITUTING THE WELFARE STATE (MENDOZA, 2014).

AGAINST THIS ALIENATION CONJUNCTURE, A COUNTER-AUSTERITY PROCESS EMERGED IN SEVERAL EUROPEAN COUNTRIES, LIKE SPAIN, PORTUGAL AND GREECE. (GIUGNI, 2015).

STATE AND MEDIA DISCOURSES

ON ONE HAND, SUCH CONFLICTS WERE NARRATED BY THE **STATE** OR THROUGH CLASSICAL **MASS MEDIA** LIKE SOME NEWSPAPERS AND TELEVISION.

HOWEVER, THESE GRAND NARRATIVES ENGENDERED AN IMPORTANT **COUNTER-HEGEMONIC DISCURSIVITY.**

SOCIAL MOVEMENTS' COUNTER-DISCOURSE

ON THE OTHER HAND, SOCIAL MOVEMENTS AND ALTERNATIVE MEDIA USE A '**RADICAL IMAGINATION**' POSTURE AGAINST AUSTERITY (HAIVE, 2014).

SUCH RADICAL IMAGINATION MAY BE ACTIVATED BY ORDINARY CITIZENS, AFFILIATED NOT ONLY TO POLITICAL PARTIES, BUT MAINLY ADHERING TO ALTERNATIVE **SOCIAL, POLITICAL AND CULTURAL MOVEMENTS AND MARGINALITIES.**

PUBLIC SPHERE PARTICIPATION

THEREFORE, THE PRESENT BOOK AIMS MOSTLY TO UNDERTAKE A STUDY OF PARTICIPATION IN THE PUBLIC SPHERE, REGARDING POLITICAL, CULTURAL AND URBAN RUPTURES AND RESISTANCE.

CONTEMPORARY CITIES ARE SPACES OF HYBRID CULTURAL PRODUCTION, THAT IS SHAPED BY GLOBALIZATION AND MIGRATION. THIS ENGENDERS PLURAL WAYS OF LIFE, DIFFERENT CULTURAL FORMS AND SINGULAR CULTURAL MEANINGS (MILES, 2007).

SUCH PRODUCTION OF CULTURAL AND POLITICAL FORMS AND MEANINGS OFTEN OCCURS THROUGH PROCESSES THAT USE BOTH *SOCIAL STORIES* AND *SOCIOLOGICAL ACCOUNTS*.

SOCIOLOGICAL ACCOUNTS

DIFFERENTLY BUT COMPLEMENTARILY, A *SOCIOLOGICAL ACCOUNT*, AND THE RESPECTIVE PLOT, ARE INTERPRETATIONS MADE BY A SOCIOLOGIST OR BY OTHER SOCIAL RESEARCHER, WITH SCIENTIFIC PURPOSES, ABOUT PARTICULAR SOCIAL STORIES / ACCOUNTS AND THE CORRESPONDENT PLOTS.

SOCIOLOGICAL ACCOUNTS MAY ARTICULATE PORTUGUESE SOCIETY AND OTHER CULTURES, THROUGH "(...) ON THE ONE HAND, INTERACTIVE DIGITAL FORMS OF INTERCULTURAL COMMUNICATION AND, ON THE OTHER, MULTIMODAL TEXTUALITIES ("HIPERTEXTUALITIES") IN THE PRODUCTION OF LUSOPHONE SENSE." (MARTINS, 2015, P. 28).

SOCIAL STORIES

A *SOCIAL STORY / ACCOUNT* IS A COLLECTION OR FUSION OF NARRATIONS, COMMENTS, OPINIONS, CRITIQUES, COMMON IDEAS AND EMOTIONS, PRODUCED BY ORDINARY SOCIAL AGENTS.

HOWEVER, DIFFERENTLY FROM SIMPLE NARRATIONS, OFTEN THEIR PLOTS COLLECTIVELY ENGENDER MORE COMPLEX NARRATIVES, LIKE CRITICAL MEANING, ETHICAL SIGNIFICATIONS, AND SOMETIMES AESTHETICAL CONNOTATIONS.

THIS IS DONE THROUGH THE TRANSLATION OF INDIVIDUAL, GROUP, CLASS, GENDER AND RACE DISCOURSES, IDEOLOGIES OR MORE GENERAL EPOCHAL ÉPISTÉMÈ, INTO COMMON SENSE DISCOURSES OR COUNTER-DISCOURSES, INVOLVED IN A SPECIFIC SOCIAL PROCESS, EVENT OR ACTION.

SOCIAL / SOCIOLOGICAL ACCOUNTABILITY

THE TWO TYPES OF ACCOUNTS AND UNDERLYING PLOTS MAY BLEND, IF THEIR OBJECTIVES ARE ARTICULATED.

THIS HAPPENS WHEN A SOCIOLOGIST WORKS IN COLLABORATION WITH COMMON SOCIAL ACTORS.

E.G. FOR TASKS AND ACTIONS THAT GO BEYOND MERE TRADITIONAL, SPECIALIZED AND SCIENTIFIC PURPOSES ISOLATED FROM THEIR SOCIAL CONTEXT, THAT IS, INCLUDING ECONOMIC, POLITICAL AND CULTURAL CRITIQUE / ENGAGEMENT.

IN SHORT, A CRITICAL *SOCIAL ACCOUNTABILITY* MUST BE ARTICULATED WITH A CRITICAL *SOCIOLOGICAL ACCOUNTABILITY*.

HYBRID ACCOUNTABILITY

SUCH **HYBRID ACCOUNTABILITY** IS FURTHER DEVELOPED THROUGH A REFLEXIVE DEVICE TYPICALLY ASSOCIATED WITH WEB 3.0 (THE SOCIAL SEMANTIC WEB): A SOCIAL / SOCIOLOGICAL ONTOLOGY.

(FOR MORE DETAILS, SEE NEXT FRAME, PAGE 32 , AND CONSULT BIBLIOGRAPHY: ANDRADE, 2011, PP. 170-172).

SOCIAL / SOCIOLOGICAL ONTOLOGY

A SOCIAL / SOCIOLOGICAL ONTOLOGY MAY BE DEFINED AS A COLLECTION OF CONCEPTS MEANINGS, ARTICULATED THROUGH LOGICAL RELATIONSHIPS, WHICH CIRCUMSCRIBES THE SOCIAL SEMANTICS OF A CERTAIN AREA OF KNOWLEDGE, CONNECTED WITH A SPECIFIC SOCIAL AND POWER ARENA.

IN THIS BOOK, AN EXAMPLE OF SUCH ONTOLOGY PERTAINS TO THE PUBLIC SPHERE WHERE CITIZEN PARTICIPATION OCCURS, AND MAY INCLUDE ANY TYPE OF MEDIA.

COMMON AND INNOVATIVE ACTIONS AND CONCEPTS

THE PRESENT BOOK, THROUGH THE IMAGES AND TEXT EXHIBITED, WILL TRY TO EXTRACT SOME OF THE **COMMON AND INNOVATIVE ACTIONS AND CONCEPTS** THAT CONSTITUTE **PUBLIC WISDOM** USED BY ORDINARY PEOPLE.

THIS OCCURS WITHIN A COUNTER-HEGEMONIC MODE OF COMMUNICATION AND COUNTER-DISCOURSE, IN ORDER TO CRITICIZE THE HEGEMONIC POWER STRATEGY OF AUSTERITY AND ITS DISCOURSES.

ALTERNATIVE COMMUNICATION

COUNTER-DISCOURSE AGAINST AUSTERITOCRACY OFTEN OPPOSES ETHICAL AND AESTHETICAL POLITICS TO UN-ETHICAL (AND SOMETIMES UN-AESTHETICAL) AUSTERITY POLICIES.

E.G., BESIDES CONCRETE ACTIONS AT URBAN SPACES SUCH AS DEMONSTRATIONS, ALTERNATIVE COMMUNICATION AND DISCOURSES MAY OPERATE THROUGH ART COMMUNICATION.

THIS IS THE CASE OF COMMUNICATING ART THROUGH DEPICTION OF MURALS AND POLITICAL POSTERS, OR BY INCLUDING TEXT AND IMAGES INSIDE DIGITAL SOCIAL NETWORKS, AMONG OTHER INSTRUMENTS FOR EXPRESSING INDIGNATION.

IN PARTICULAR, GENDER AS AN ALTERNATIVE ARENA IN THE AGE OF AUSTERITY, IS CONTEXTUALIZED BY OUR MEDIA CULTURE IN CURIOUS MODES (SEE BIBLIOGRAPHY: NEGRA, 2014).

HYBRID RHETORICS AND HERMENEUTICS

MOREOVER, THROUGH THE APPLICATION OF SOCIOLOGICAL COMICS, IT IS POSSIBLE TO RECONSTRUCT AND PUBLICIZE PRACTICES, INTERPRETATIONS AND EXPLANATIONS OF URBAN STRUGGLES OR OTHER PUBLIC SPHERE PHENOMENA IN A HYBRID WAY.

THAT IS, THROUGH THE FUSION OF **RHETORICS** (ARGUMENTATIONS) AND **HERMENEUTICS** (INTERPRETATIONS) LOCATED SOMEWHERE BETWEEN SCIENCE, NEW MEDIA AND ART.

THE 3 CENTRAL MODES OF COMMUNICATION

SUCH DIVERSE STRATEGIES FOR COMMUNICATING COLLECTIVE AND ETHICAL/AESTHETICAL MEANINGS, ARE ORGANIZED ACCORDING TO 3 MAIN **MODES OF COMMUNICATION** OPERATING WITHIN CONTEMPORANEITY:

1. **CO-PRESENCE COMMUNICATION**, E.G. MURALS, GRAFFITI, ART STENCILS, POLITICAL DEMONSTRATIONS;

2. **CLASSICAL MASS MEDIA** LIKE NEWSPAPERS AND TELEVISION;

3. **DIGITAL MEDIA** SUCH AS DIGITAL SOCIAL NETWORKS.

1.2. QUESTIONS and HYPOTHESIS

1ST QUESTION:

HOW **SOCIAL MOVEMENTS** USE THE 3 MODES OF COMMUNICATION TO ENHANCE CITIZENS PARTICIPATION WITHIN **COUNTER-AUSTERITY**?

1ST HYPOTHESIS (SEE ALSO PAGE 13):

AFTER EXPERIMENTING A DISENCHANTEMENT WITH POLITICAL PARTIES, CITIZENS ARE TRYING TO INNOVATE, BY INVENTING NEW STRATEGIES OF POLITICAL ACTION.

THIS IS FORGED WITH **INDIGNATION** AND SOMETIMES **VIOLENCE**, ARTICULATED WITH **ETHICS**, AND OFTEN USING **AESTHETICAL MEANS** AND METHODS, LIKE PUBLIC ART INSTALLATIONS AND PERFORMANCES.

2ND QUESTION:

INVERSELY, HOW CAN THE **NATURE OF COMMUNICATION** INFLUENCE SOCIAL MOVEMENTS TO DEVELOP **COUNTER-AUSTERITY**?

2ND HYPOTHESIS (SEE ALSO PAGE 19):

WITHIN CONTEMPORARY SOCIETIES, DIVERSE MEDIA ARE NOT JUST BEING SIMPLY ARTICULATED AMONG THEM, LIKE IN HYPERMEDIA, BUT ALSO MIXED IN NOVEL WAYS.

E.G, MEDIA DIFFERENT IN NATURE FROM THE PRECEDENT ONES, NAMED **HYBRIMEDIA**, ARE USED EXTENSIVELY IN **COUNTER-AUSTERITY** PROCESSES.

3RD QUESTION:

HOW **DIGITAL SOCIAL NETWORKS** ALLOW AND ENHANCE SOCIAL COOPERATION AND **COUNTER-AUSTERITY**?

3RD HYPOTHESIS (SEE ALSO PAGE 21):

DIGITAL SOCIAL NETWORKS (THE SO-CALLED **WEB 2.0**) MAY HAVE A CENTRAL ROLE IN URBAN STRUGGLES, BY GATHERING HUGE CROWDS WITHIN A COMMON GLOBAL FRONT.

AND SOCIAL SEMANTIC NETWORKS (ALSO NAMED **WEB 3.0**, SEE ANDRADE, 2011) TRANSFORM POLITICAL INFORMATION INTO DEMOCRATIC **KNOWLEDGE** ON **COUNTER-AUSTERITY**.

4TH QUESTION:

HOW **EXPERIMENTAL BOOKS** MAY CONTRIBUTE TO THE DEVELOPMENT OF SCIENTIFIC MEDIA FOR CULTURAL CITIZENSHIP AND **COUNTER-AUSTERITY**?

4TH HYPOTHESIS (DEMONSTRATED WITHIN THIS WHOLE BOOK):

SOCIOLOGICAL COMICS IS AN EXPERIMENTAL BOOK GENRE, THAT FOCUS ON SOCIAL DISSEMINATION OF INFORMATION AND KNOWLEDGE IN WAYS THAT MAY ENHANCE SCIENTIFIC AND POLITICAL LITERACIES ON **COUNTER-AUSTERITY**.

FOR INSTANCE: THROUGH OPEN ACCESS, VISUAL AND DIGITAL LANGUAGES, INTERMEDIA, TRANSMEDIA, HYBRIMEDIA, ETC.-).

2. SOCIAL STORIES/SOCIOLOGICAL ACCOUNTS AS PUBLIC SPHERE PARTICIPATION

2.1. CO-PRESENCE COMMUNICATION

RECENT **SOCIAL PORTUGUESE CONTEXT** OF AUSTERITY MAY BE ACCOUNTED BY AND FOR CITIZENS, WITHIN PUBLIC SPACE, THROUGH ART

E.G. MURALS WORK AS **SOCIAL PLOTS**, AS THEY COMMUNICATE MEANING, IN A NARRATIVE WAY, TO CITIZENS IN CO-PRESENCE WITH CITY WALLS

AS FOR THE SOCIOLOGIST, HE USES **SOCIOLOGIC PLOTS** WHEN HE INTERPRETS MURALS OR OTHER ART GENRES AS ICONIC STORIES ACCOUNTED BY CITIZENS

SOCIAL / SOCIOLOGICAL ACCOUNT 1: **A POLITICAL MURAL MAKING**

THIS MURAL WAS PAINTED AT A CENTRAL LISBON AREA, IN THE NAMED 'WALL OF FAME'

THIS IS A PLACE WHERE POLITICAL MURALS AND GRAFFITI SHARE GOOD PUBLIC VISIBILITY

FORMER PRIME-
MINISTER OF
PORTUGAL,
PEDRO PASSOS
COELHO
(2011-2015)

FORMER VICE
PRIME-
MINISTER OF
PORTUGAL,
PAULO PORTAS

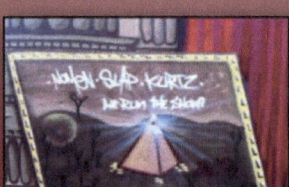

THIS MURAL IS A
DIRECT AND
CRITICAL ACCOUNT
OF THE UNETHICAL
DEPENDENCY OF
PORTUGUESE STATE
TO AUSTERITY
**EUROPEAN
POLICIES**

MEANING:
'HOW MUCH LONGER DO
YOU WANT TO WATCH THIS
SHOW? OUR **DEBT**
KEEPS GROWING!'

SOCIAL/ SOCIOLOGICAL ACCOUNT 2: SOME **ANTECEDENTS OF THE PRESENT CRISIS** ARE ACCOUNTED THROUGH ART STENCILS AND OTHER POLITICAL AESTHETICS

HISTORY IS A COLLECTION OF ACCOUNTED AND UNACCOUNTED STORIES

THIS MEANS: 'UGLY AND BAD POLITICIANS'

IN THE LAST DECADES, POLITICIANS AND OTHER HEGEMONIC SOCIAL AGENTS AND PROCESSES WERE DISQUALIFIED BY CITIZENS AT PUBLIC SPACES, E.G. THROUGH LANGUAGE GAMES (A WITTGENSTEIN'S CONCEPT RETAKEN BY HABERMAS TO APPLY IT TO COMMUNICATIVE ACTION)

= 'MAKE A DIET!'

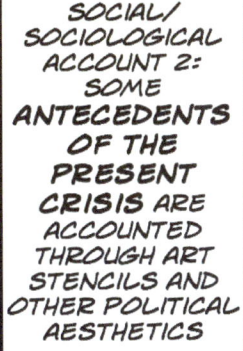

SOME POLITICAL AND ETHIC TARGETS ARE FOOTBALL, FASCISM ...

= 'DADDY TAUGHT ME'

OR A CROSS USED AS A SEX SYMBOL BY SOME PRIESTS ...

INDIGNATION IS DEPICTED IN DIVERSE MODES:

= 'WAKE UP PORTUGAL!'

WITHIN MARXIST TRADITION REVISITED: 2 STEPS BACK/1 MAYBE 2 FORWARD...

THROUGH MEMORY OF 25 APRIL PORTUGUESE REVOLUTION: FLOWERS AND GUNS...

CONVOKING ANTI-GLOBALIZATION MOVEMENTS AND SLOGANS

APPEALS TO DIRECT ACTION

= 'REVOLT'

EVEN USING RELIGION ..

OR, BEYOND REVELATION, REVOLUTION

10

DEMONSTRATION IS AN ACCOUNT TACTIC AND AN ART FORM WORKING AT THE PUBLIC SPHERE. NEXT PAGES SHOW SOME SCENES AT A DEMONSTRATION AGAINST AUSTERITY THAT OCCURED IN LISBON, PORTUGAL, THE 2ND MARCH 2013.

SOCIAL/SOCIOLOGICAL ACCOUNT 3: THIS IS A DEMONSTRATION ACCOUNTED WITH PHOTOGRAPHS BY A SOCIOLOGIST

THE SOCIOLOGIST MAY BE AN ENGAGED CITIZEN AND SOMETIMES AN AUTHOR'S HETERONYM... SOCIOLOGIST JOSÉ OLIVEIRA ALLOWED THIS BOOK'S AUTHOR TO PUBLISH HIS SOCIOLOGICAL PHOTOS DEPICTING THE DEMONSTRATION EVENT

POLITICS IS WEARABLE

GILLYFLOWERS REMEMBERING APRIL 1974 REVOLUTION

DISABLED PEOPLE ALSO GO FOR A PUBLIC RIDE

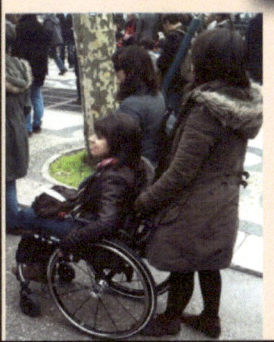

SOME CITIZENS INTERPRET POLITICIANS AS UNETHICAL BEINGS WITH DEFICIENT VISION (OR ASSHOLES...)

A DOG AND HIS PET, THE FORMER MINISTER OF PARLAMENTARY AFFAIRS JOSÉ RELVAS, BACK IN 2013 ...

'RESIGNATION NOW!'

MEANING: 'VAMPIRES ATTACK ONLY IN THE SILENCE'

3 GENERATIONS ARE PRESENT: A CHILD WITH A MEGAPHONE ON HIS FATHER SHOULDERS, AND RETIRED PEOPLE FIGHTING AGAINST PENSIONS TAXATION

= 'ROLL, SPIN, TRUNDLE, LIFT, REVOLT'

THIS IS ANOTHER POPULAR LANGUAGE GAME

COMMON CONNOTATION: 'OUT!'

12

SOCIOLOGICAL HYPOTHESES ARE TESTABLE (THAT IS, FOUNDED TRUE/ CONFIRMED OR WRONG/INFIRMED), AMONG OTHER METHODS, THROUGH STREET DEMONSTRATION...

HYPOTHESIS 1 TO TEST (SEE RESPECTIVE QUESTION AT PAGE 6):

AFTER EXPERIMENTING A DISENCHANTMENT WITH POLITICAL PARTIES, CITIZENS ARE TRYING TO INNOVATE, BY INVENTING NEW STRATEGIES OF POLITICAL ACTION MADE WITH INDIGNATION AND ETHICS, THAT OFTEN USE AESTHETICAL MEANS AND METHODS, LIKE PUBLIC ART, INSTALLATIONS AND PERFORMANCES

= 'GET OUT!'

= 'PSD, FMI, PS, CDS CORRUPTION'

IN THIS POSTER, SOME PORTUGUESE POLITICAL PARTIES ARE ACCUSED OF CORRUPTION, REPRESENTED THROUGH A POLITICAL 'WORLD/ BURDEN' THAT COMMON PEOPLE HAS TO 'CARRY'

= 'I'M FED UP WITH FRAUDS'

POSTERS DEPICTED BY EACH CITIZEN PUBLICIZE A LOCAL PUBLIC OPINION, FORGED IN THE LOCAL/GLOBAL PUBLIC SPHERE

= 'DEMOCRISY VERSUS HYPOCRACY'

= ' – TAXES +PROGRESS'

THIS IS AN ELOQUENT COMMON CITIZEN LANGUAGE GAME, A SUFFIX SWAP INSIDE THE WORDS 'DEMOCRACY' AND 'HYPOCRISY'

= 'SINTRA IN STRUGGLE AGAINST EXPLOITATION AND UNEMPLOYMENT, PORTUGAL HAS A FUTURE'

A WHOLE TOWN, SINTRA, AS A PROTEST AGENT IN THE DIALOGIC PUBLIC SPHERE

= 'PARTY FOR ANIMALS AND NATURE'

PARLIAMENTARY AND NON-PARLAMENTARY PARTIES JOINED THIS DEMONSTRATION

THE FORMER PRIME MINISTER, REPRESENTED BY A RABBIT, WAS SYMBOLICALLY HANGED (HIS FAMILY NAME IS COELHO' = 'RABBIT') THROUGH THIS PRACTICE OF COMMUNICATIVE ACTION AND COUNTER-DISCOURSE

= 'IN MY BANK I KEEP THE HUNGER OF YOUR CHILDREN'

EVERY PLACE AND SOCIAL-SYMBOLIC METHODS ARE USED TO CALL ATTENTION TO INDIGNATION

POLITICIANS 'MUSIC' IS ALREADY KNOWN...

=
'ENOUGH, OBVIOUSLY YOU MUST RESIGN'

'BE AWARE OF PICKPOCKETS! [THE FORMER PRIME MINISTER AND THE FORMER FINANCE MINISTER, VÍTOR GASPAR]

2.2. MASS MEDIA COMMUNICATION

BEFORE THE DEMONSTRATION, NEWSPAPER 'PÚBLICO' DID A POLL, ASKING: 'ARE YOU GOING TO THE DEMONSTRATION NEXT SATURDAY (...)?' (ANSWERS: 59% YES, 41% NO)

SOCIAL/SOCIOLOGICAL ACCOUNT 4: THE DAY AFTER = LISBON DEMONSTRATION 'BIOGRAPHY' WAS ACCOUNTED BY NEWSPAPER 'PÚBLICO', THE 3 MARCH 2013. IN OTHER WORDS: THE LIFE STORY OF THE EVENTS AT THE 2ND MARCH DEMONSTRATION IN LISBON, WAS FOLLOWED HOUR BY HOUR.

FOR EXAMPLE:

= '14H 35' DEMONSTRATION DEPARTS FROM MARQUÊS DE POMBAL SQUARE TOWARDS TERREIRO DO PAÇO SQ. THIS PLACE WAS CHOSEN BECAUSE HERE ARE LOCATED MANY HEAD OFFICES OF GOVERNMENT ADMINISTRATION'

= 'TODAY I AM IN THE STREET, TOMORROW YOU ARE' [OUT] ['RUA' MEANS 'STREET' AND ALSO 'OUT' IN PORTUGUESE]

LISBON CITY HALL DIDN'T REMOVE STONES NEAR THE MEETING SPOT, AS PROMISSED BY ITS INSTITUTIONAL DISCOURSE

= '14:13 PROTESTERS --- PAINT POSTERS'

15H 08' A READER SENDS A PHOTO FROM THE STREET EVENT TO A NEWSPAPER

17

15H 27'

= 'THERE IS NO ECONOMY WITHOUT PEOPLE!'

NÃO HÁ ECONOMIA SEM PESSOAS!

= 'DON'T ROB MY FUTURE'

NÃO ME ROUBEM O FUTURO!

16H 05'

= 'DON'T TROIK ME'

NÃO ME TROIKEM!

16H 42': ANOTHER POLITICAL LANGUAGE GAME WITHIN COMMUNICATIVE ACTION

17H 46' FEMINISTS AND ECOLOGISTS, ANONYMOUS MOVEMENT, ETC, PUBLICIZE THEIR COUNTER-DISCOURSE

17H 59 A NEW SUGGESTED FACE FOR THE PORTUGUESE REPUBLIC

NOTE THIS 'COMMON CONCEPT', INVENTED WITHIN URBAN STRUGGLES

= 'THIS IS AN AUSTERICÍDIO' [MEANING KILLING THROUGH AUSTERITY']

20H 23' THE FIRST TIME IN A DEMONSTRATION...

= 'THIS GOVERNMENT GAVE ME THE GIFT TO TRANSFORM ME INTO A REVOLUTIONARY...'

SOCIAL/SOCIOLOGICAL ACCOUNT 5: INDIVIDUAL LIFE ACCOUNTS.

IN THE SAME DAY 3 MARCH, NEWSPAPER 'PÚBLICO' PUBLISHED VIDEO INTERVIEWS INCLUDING AN INQUIRY ON EXPECTATIONS OF YOUNG PEOPLE ABOUT UNEMPLOYMENT AND EMIGRATION. THIS QUESTION: 'ONE IDEA FOR PORTUGAL', WAS ASKED TO PROFESSIONALS BELONGING TO SEVERAL SOCIAL CLASSES

18

SOCIAL/ SOCIOLOGICAL ACCOUNT 6: **HYBRIMEDIA TALES**

(SOURCE; NEWSPAPER 'PÚBLICO', THE 3 MARCH 2013)

HYPOTHESIS 2 TO TEST (SEE CONNECTED QUESTION 2 IN PAGE 6):

IN CONTEMPORARY SOCIETIES, DIVERSE MEDIA ARE NOT JUST BEING ARTICULATED AS IN HYPERMEDIA, BUT MIXED IN NEW WAYS, PRODUCING HYBRIDIZED MEDIA, ORIGINAL IN THEIR VERY NATURE, OFTEN CALLED **HYBRIMEDIA**

FOR EXAMPLE, THE CASE OF **VIDEOS** THAT ARE INSERTED IN **ONLINE VERSIONS** OF A **NEWSPAPER**, SUCH AS 'PÚBLICO'

"A minha dor é uma arma"

Recorde o dia, minuto a minuto

Manifestações de sábado com pouco eco na imprensa internacional

PSP liberta dois manifestantes detidos no Porto sem os acusar

SOMETIMES, HYPERMEDIA TELL A **META-ACCOUNT**. E.G. WHEN A NEWSPAPER NARRATES A SOCIAL CONTEXT THAT WAS ALREADY TOLD THROUGH ANOTHER MEDIUM, SUCH AS A POSTER

THIS IS THE CASE OF SOME VIRTUAL POSTERS THAT APPEARED IN DIGITAL SOCIAL NETWORKS, THAT USED KNOWN AUTHORS TO 'COMMENT' OR 'CRITICIZE' THE PORTUGUESE CRISIS. LATER, SUCH POSTERS WERE REFERRED BY NEWSPAPER 'PÚBLICO' WITHIN A NEW ACCOUNT...

A POSTER WITH VICTOR HUGO CITES THIS WRITER'S ACCOUNT: 'UTOPIA TODAY, MEAT AND BONES TOMORROW'

JOHN STEINBECK: 'IN THE PEOPLE SOUL, THE GRAPES OF WRATH GROW, ROBUST, FOR HARVEST'

IN THIS POSTER'S ACCOUNT PICTURING EINSTEIN, THE ENERGY OF PROTESTERS IS RELATED TO SOCIAL MASSES

OTHER MEDIA WERE HYBRIDIZED WITHIN THE ACCOUNTS OF PROTEST, AS COMICS AND COLLAGES

YET ANOTHER CASE OF META-ACCOUNT IS THE STORY TOLD BY MURALS THAT, IN A SECOND MOVE, IS WRITTEN BY A NEWSPAPER

OR AN ACCOUNT PRESENTED BY A NEWSPAPER THAT WAS PREVIOUSLY PUBLISHED BY DIGITAL SOCIAL MEDIA: INFORMING THAT '(...) EVERYTHING IS READY FOR THE DEMONSTRATION'

20

SOCIAL/SOCIOLOGICAL ACCOUNT 7: A SOCIAL MOVEMENT QUEST

HYPOTHESIS 3 TO TEST (SEE RESPECTIVE QUESTION 3 IN PAGE 6): DIGITAL SOCIAL NETWORKS (THE SO-CALLED WEB 2.0) AND SOCIAL SEMANTIC NETWORKS (ALSO NAMED WEB 3.0) MAY HAVE A CENTRAL ROLE IN URBAN STRUGGLES:

THEY MAY GATHER HUGE CROWDS WITHIN A COMMON GLOBAL FRONT IN ORDER TO TRANSFORM INFORMATION INTO KNOWLEDGE ON RESISTANCE AGAINST AUSTERITY...

(SOURCE: FACEBOOK PAGE OF SOCIAL MOVEMENT 'QUE SE LIXE A TROIKA' = TO HELL WITH TROIKA, SEE BIBLIOGRAPHY)

2.3. DIGITAL COMMUNICATION

THE 21 JANUARY 2013, IN THIS SOCIAL NETWORK, A DEMONSTRATION IS CONVOKED FOR 2 MARCH: 'AGAINST THIS WAVE THAT DESTROYS ALL, WE WILL FILL THE STREETS WITH OUR INDIGNATION- GOVERNMENT DEMISSION, LET THE PEOPLE DECIDE THEIR LIFE...'

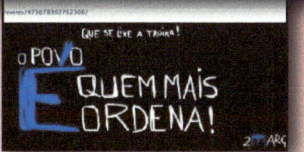

THERE WAS 24.225 PERSONS WHO SAID THEY WOULD BE PRESENT, 9661 'MAYBE'. THIS WAY OF GATHERING FRIENDS AND INVOLVING THEM TO PARTICIPATE, THROUGH 'LIKES' AND COMMENTING INFORMATION, ARE ALL TRAITS OF **WEB 2.0** SOCIAL NETWORKS.

E.G., WITHIN NEXT POSTS, THE MOVEMENT'S **TARGET AUDIENCE** IS CLARIFIED: = 'TO ALL CITIZENS WITH OR WITHOUT PARTY, EMPLOYMENT, HOPE, WE APPEAL TO JOIN US- TO ALL POLITICAL AND MILITARY ORGANIZATIONS, CIVIC MOVEMENTS, UNIONS, PARTIES, COLLECTIVITIES, INFORMAL GROUPS...'

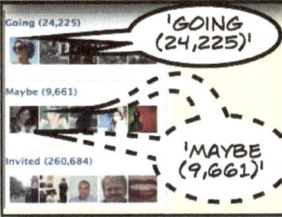

'GOING (24,225)'

'MAYBE (9,661)'

BESIDES THAT, THIS FACEBOOK WALL SPECIFIED DETAILS ON THE REASONS FOR THE STRUGGLE. AND A MAP FOR THE MEETING WAS PUBLICIZED HERE BY THE ORGANIZERS.

THIS ILLUSTRATES AN EXPLANATORY POSTURE THAT CHARACTERIZES SOCIAL SEMANTIC NETWORKS THAT CONSTITUTE **WEB 3.0.** THEY ARE NETWORKS THAT NOT ONLY CONVEY AND COMMENT INFORMATION, BUT ALSO, AND MAINLY, TRANSFORM INFORMATION INTO KNOWLEDGE, E.G. THROUGH PROFOUND DISCUSSIONS, WHICH ARE ESSENTIAL FOR POLITICAL STRUGGLES.

THE 22 JANUARY 2013, THE MOVEMENT'S **ORGANIZATION** ESTABLISHED CONTACTS (THROUGH WEB SITES, ETC.) IN ALL MAIN PORTUGUESE CITIES AND ABROAD.

'REMEMBER ... SEPTEMBER'. THIS POST REFERS TO A 2012 DEMONSTRATION, ORGANIZED AS WELL BY MOVEMENT 'TO HELL WITH TROIKA', THAT HAD AN HUGE IMPACT IN PORTUGUESE POLITICAL LIFE

Remember, remember... the 15th of September!

A MOVEMENT'S **MANIFEST** WAS PRESENTED AT **DIGITAL PUBLIC SPHERE**, WITHIN THIS SITE: = 'CRIMINAL AUSTERITY COMMANDED BY TROIKA AND HIS GOVERNMENTS INVADES ... OUR SOCIETY, RIGHTS, SCHOOLS, WATER, CULTURE, ART AND LIVES...'

MANIFEST'S COMPLETE TEXT AND USERS' LIKES, COMMENTS AND SHARES:

MANY **CITIES** ANSWERED TO THIS APPEAL, PUBLICIZING POSTERS WITH CALLS TO PUBLIC PARTICIPATION.

SOME TRANSMITTED A SYMBOLIC FORCE: GRÂNDOLA IS A REFERENCE FOR POLITICAL STRUGGLES IN PORTUGAL, AS IT IS THE NAME OF A MUSIC THAT GAVE THE SIGNAL, AT THE RADIO, FOR INITIATING 25 APRIL 1974 REVOLUTION

MARINHA GRANDE IS A TOWN WITH A TRADITION OF WORKERS STRUGGLES DURING THE FORMER FASCIST REGIME

OTHER SYMBOLIC ARGUMENT AT A FACEBOOK POST (13 FEBRUARY) WAS THE REFERENCE TO HUMBERTO DELGADO, A RESISTANT TO FORMER DICTATOR SALAZAR, WHO ORDERED HIS MURDER IN THIS SAME DAY, BACK IN 1965

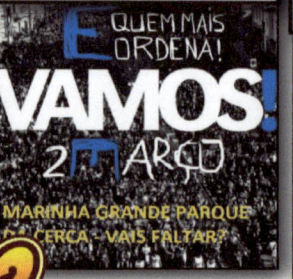

SOCIAL ACCOUNT 8 :
THE **ORDEAL OF NEW PROTEST STRATEGIES.**
SOME ARE RECENT, LIKE THE '**MARÉ**' (=TIDE).
THIS TORRENT METAPHOR MEANS A WAVE MADE BY ALL INDIGNATED PEOPLE, REGARDLESS THEIR PARTIES OR OTHER SOCIAL GROUP FIDELITY. MANY 'TIDES' WERE PUBLISHED AT 'TO HELL TO TROIKA'S FACEBOOK PAGE, IN THE LAST DAYS OF JANUARY AND BEGINNING OF FEBRUARY 2013

EACH 'MARÉ' CHOSE A PLACE TO MEET AT 2 MARCH DEMONSTRATION, BEFORE JOINING THE MAIN CROWD

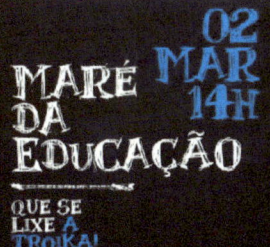

'MARÉS' OF EDUCATION WERE SOME OF THE MOST DYNAMIC ONES

STREET POSTERS WERE ARTICULATED WITH SOCIAL NETWORK POSTS (HERE, 14.2.2013)

= 'COUNTRY WITHOUT CULTURE, PEOPLE WITHOUT VOICE'

'MARÉ' OF CULTURE

MARGINALIZED AGENTS ORGANIZED AS WELL THEIR TIDES, AS 'RAINBOW MARÉ', THAT RALLIED GAYS, LESBIANS AND TRASNSEXUAL

HERE, A GRAPHIC SYMBOL FROM HUMAN RIGHTS TIDE...

OR 'DISABLED INDIGNATED PEOPLE' MARÉ

= 'A DIGNIFIED LIFE FOR ALL!'

IN PORTUGUESE, DISABLED PEOPLE CAN BE TRANSLATED BY 'DEFICIENT'. THIS POSTER SUPPRESSED THE LETTER 'D' TO TRANSFORM 'DEFICIENTES' IN 'EFICIENTES' (= 'EFFICIENT' IN ENGLISH) CITIZENS

OTHER 'TIDE' GATHERED RETIRED PEOPLE

ANOTHER FORM OF PROTEST AGAINST AUSTERITY WAS THE INTERVENTION THE 15/2 AT THE ASSEMBLY OF THE REPUBLIC, THE PORTUGUESE MAIN LEGISLATIVE ORGAN

SPANISH NEWSPAPER 'EL PAIS' ACCOUNTED THIS EVENT: REVOLUTIONARY SONG 'GRÂNDOLA' WAS PERFORMED BY THE AUDIENCE (SOURCE: POST AT 'TO HELL WITH TROIKA', 16-2-2013

OTHER TACTICS OF ACCOUNTABILITY: PROTEST AT THE 'CLUB OF THINKERS', IN OPORTO, AGAINST THE PRESENCE OF THE FORMER MINISTER OF PARLIAMENTARY AFFAIRS (18-2-2013)

HYBRIMEDIA ACCOUNTING MEANS TO ACCOUNT USING HYBRIDIZED MEDIA, E.G. AT SOCIAL NETWORKS: HERE, A VIDEO ENTITLED 'REVOLUTION NOW' BLENDS WITH A FACEBOOK POST, WHERE POLITICAL SITUATION IS COMMENTED.

= 'DON'T BEAR IT ANYMORE!'

BELOW, ANOTHER ACCOUNTING TACTIC USING A FACEBOOK POST: IT ADVERTISES THAT MINISTERS SHOULD BE CHASED BY PEOPLE SINGING THE SONG 'GRÂNDOLA' UNTIL THE 2 MARCH DEMONSTRATION. AFTER THE MESSAGE, THIS REALLY HAPPENED IN SEVERAL EVERYDAY SITUATIONS.

24

SOCIAL/
SOCIOLOGICAL
ACCOUNT 9:
CITIZENS/
INSTITUTIONS
PREPARING FOR
DEMONSTRATION

BY THE MIDDLE-END
OF FEBRUARY 2013,
MULTIPLE VOICES
SENT PUBLIC
APPEALS TO
PARTICIPATION IN THE
2 MARCH
DEMONSTRATION, TO
TRANSFORM IT IN AN
HISTORICAL EVENT

A KNOWN ACTRESS
CALL THE 19
FEBRUARY: 154
LIKED, 24
COMMENTED, 212
SHARED...

= 'I WILL
BE IN THE
STREET THE 2
MARCH. AND
YOU?'

19 FEBRUARY: THE
REVOLUTIONARY
SONG 'GRÂNDOLA',
SANG IN FINNISH BY
'AGIT PROP GROUP',
IS SHARED IN
SOCIAL NETWORKS

20 FEBRUARY:
UNIVERSITARY
STUDENTS
CONSTITUTE A SITE TO
PROPAGATE
DEMONSTRATION
ANNOUNCEMENTS

24 FEBRUARY: GESTURAL
LANGUAGE INTERPRETER
APPEALS TO DEAFS AND
MUTES TO EXPRESS THE
SOUND OF THEIR
APPARENT SILENCE.
NOBODY IS LEFT OUT...

20 FEBRUARY:
MOBILIZATION TO
PAINT A COLLECTIVE
MURAL TO ANNOUNCE
2 MARCH
DEMONSTRATION

376 LIKED; 50
COMMENTED; 650
SHARED

MOBILIZAÇÃO PARA
A PINTURA DE MURAL
RUA MARQUÊS DE FRONTEIRA / DOM. 24 FEV 14H

21/2/2013: A CITIZEN
APPEAL AT FACEBOOK ...

AND A COMMENT ON
THIS POST...

= 'I AM
GOING, WITH MY
KIDS, HUSBAND,
FRIENDS .. I WOULD LIKE
TO SEE ALL UNIONS AND
PARTIES FROM RIGHT
TO LEFT'S
FLAGS...'

25

24 FEBRUARY: A 'MARE' IN
SPAIN, WHERE THIS FORM
OF PROTEST WAS BORN,
THE 5 MAI 2011. SOCIAL
NETWORKS GLOBALLY
ACCOUNT THE EVENT. THE
MOVEMENT BECOMES
INTERNATIONAL,
PLANETARY AND LOCAL/
GLOBAL.

(fotografia Borja Sánchez Trillo – AFP)

25 FEBRUARY: A MURAL ANNOUNCING THE DEMONSTRATION IS PAINTED COLLECTIVELY

Que se Lixe a Troika! Queremos as nossas Vidas
February 25

Esclarecimento

Sobre "procedimentos rotineiros" levados a cabo por "agentes de segurança pública":

Código de Processo Penal 250°, n.ºs 1 e 2
...

25 FEBRUARY: SOCIAL NETWORKS WARN ABOUT POSSIBLE 'ROUTINE PROCEDURES' BY THE POLICE

COUNTER-DISCOURSE THE 25 FEBRUARY: AT PORTUGUESE SOCIETY OF AUTHORS, A WRITER, AT AN AWARD CEREMONY, READS HIS SPEECH WRITTEN IN THE BACK OF A FLYER, THAT BECOMES VISIBLE TO THE AUDIENCE. HE DIDN'T RECEIVE HIS LITERATURE AWARD...

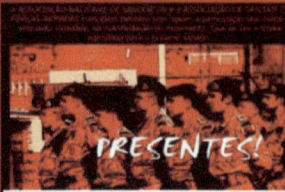

PRESENTES!

25 FEBRUARY: MILITARY PROFESSIONAL ASSOCIATIONS PUBLISH THEIR ADHESION TO 2 MARCH DEMONSTRATION

= 'INITIATIVE FOR A CITIZEN AUDITING TO THE PUBLIC DEBT'

2M | LISBOA
Iniciativa por Uma Auditoria Cidadã
Dívida Pública junta-se ao protest

A todas as organizações políticas militares, movimentos cívicos, partido
apelam

FACEBOOK, 26/2

A IAC vai ao 2
Auditoria Cida
Dívida
auditoriacidad

nossas Vidas
February 26

2M | FIAR marca presença

Dia 2 de Março estamos na RUA!
contra o sufocar da cultura e das artes; contra os cortes na educação; contra a destruição do serviço de saúde; contra o fim dos direitos laborais; contra políticas que desrepeitam o...See More

FIAR

FACEBOOK, 26/2: THE CENTER FOR THE STREET ARTS SAYS IT WILL BE ON THE STREET THE 2 MARCH

28/2: 'ANGRY PEOPLE': THIS IS A POLITICAL 'DETOUR' OF A POPULAR COMPUTER GAME ('ANGRY BIRDS') AT A SOCIAL NETWORK, SHOWING POLITICIANS DEPICTED AS GAME CHARACTERS. THE GAME'S NAME 'ANGRY BIRDS' IS TRANSFORMED INTO A BIG POLITICAL GAME: 'ANGRY PEOPLE! [PEOPLE= 'POVO', IN PORTUGUESE]

28/2: DESIGNERS AND ARTISTS ANNOUNCE THAT THEY WILL BE AT THE DEMONSTRATION TO MAKE POSTERS FOR P(R)O(TE)STERS

THIS SPEECH, MADE AT THE URBAN PUBLIC SPHERE BY A CHILD AGAINST HUNGER, IS APPEALING FOR RADICAL CHANGE

A DIGITAL COMMUNICATION SYMBOL ('LIKE') IS ASSOCIATED WITH A CO-PRESENCE SYMBOL (THE STREET = RUA)

= 'LIKE THE STREET'

= 'IT IS MORE LEGITIMATE TO PARTICIPATE IN THIS PROTEST THAN TO VOTE...'

2 MARCH IN THE MORNING. A DEMONSTRATION'S ARCHIVE AND MEMORY : CALL FOR PHOTOS OF THE DEMONSTRATIONS AROUND THE WORLD SUPPORTING PORTUGAL STRUGGLE, TO BE PUBLISHED AT A SITE

SOCIAL/ SOCIOLOGICAL ACCOUNT 10:

THE MOMENT OF TRUTH: 2 MARCH DEMONSTRATION

THIS IS A MOMENT WHEN CONTACTS AT SOCIAL NETWORKS BECAME FRENETIC

AT LISBON, SOMEONE AT FACEBOOK SUGGESTS TO CHANGE THE NAME OF TERREIRO DO PAÇO SQUARE (= 'PALACE SQUARE') INTO 'PEOPLE SQUARE'

'2,037 LIKES' ON THIS

SINCE THE BEGINNING OF THIS MEETING, SEVERAL FLOWS FROM DIFFERENT 'MARÉS' CONVERGE TO THE DEMONSTRATION SITE, AND ARE PUBLISHED IN FACEBOOK IN REAL TIME

THE DEMONSTRATION ITINERARY MAP WAS CIRCULATING WITHIN SOCIAL NETWORKS

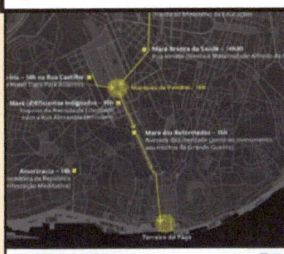

EVENT ORGANIZERS AND TV STATIONS REPORT: = 'THE BIGGEST DEMONSTRATION EVER AT OPORTO: 400 THOUSAND PEOPLE IN THE STREETS!'

AT LISBON, SOME ESTIMATE THAT 800 THOUSAND WERE ACHIEVED ...

A MOTION OF CENSURE CLAIMING GOVERNMENT DEMISSION IS READ AT TERREIRO DO PAÇO SQ.

A POET AND SINGER READS A PROTEST POEM

A WOMAN SENDS A LETTER TO THE FORMER PRESIDENT OF REPUBLIC ANIBAL CAVACO SILVA, WITH A CHECK OF JUST 9 EUROS THAT SHE RECEIVED AS AN UNEMPLOYMENT COMPENSATION, WHICH SHE CONSIDERS TO BE AN INSULT

AT PARIS, PORTUGUESE CITIZENS EXPRESS THEIR WILL TO RETURN TO A BETTER PORTUGAL

7 MARCH POST ON THE OFFICIAL FACE/ POSTURE FROM THE FORMER PRESIDENT OF THE REPUBLIC CAVACO SILVA: ALWAYS SMILING AND MUTE REACTIONS REGARDING RECENT DEMONSTRATIONS

AT LONDON, NEAR THE PORTUGUESE EMBASSY, A SOLIDARITY MEETING TAKES PLACE

= 'BY NOW IT SEEMS THERE ISN'T DANGER'

= 'BUT THE TIDE IS RISING...'

3. CONCLUSIONS
DERIVED FROM TESTED HYPOTHESIS

1ST CONCLUSION
(SEE RESPECTIVE QUESTION 1 AND HYPOTHESIS 1 AT PAGES 6 AND 13)

IN THE LAST DECADES, *SOCIAL MOVEMENTS* ARE EXTENSIVELY USING NOVEL STRATEGIES FOR CONDUCTING POLITICAL ACTION, E.G. WHEN FORGING *COUNTER-AUSTERITY*.

IN FACT, THE RIGHT FOR INDIGNATION AGAINST *AUSTERITOCRACY*, REPRESENTED BY *AUSTERITY POLICIES AND POLITICS*, IS EXTERIORIZED NOWADAYS AT THE PUBLIC SPHERE THROUGH ORIGINAL STRATEGIES SUCH AS '*TIDES*', BESIDES THE CLASSICAL POLITICAL GAMES.

'TIDES' ARE PROTEST PROCESSES INCLUDING THE PARTICIPATION OF SOCIAL AGENTS BELONGING TO MULTIPLE MARGINALIZED SOCIAL CLASSES, PROFESSIONS, RETIRED PEOPLE, UNEMPLOYED YOUNGSTERS, WOMEN, GAYS AND LESBIANS, AND MANY OTHER SOCIAL FRAGMENTATIONS.

2ND CONCLUSION
(SEE CORRESPONDENT QUESTION 2 AND HYPOTHESIS 2 AT PAGES 6 AND 19)

COMMUNICATION PHENOMENA INFLUENCES SOCIAL PROCESSES IN GENERAL, AND SOCIAL MOVEMENTS IN PARTICULAR, LIKE THE ONES CLAIMING FOR *COUNTER-AUSTERITY* THROUGH SINGULAR HYBRID TACTICS AND PRACTISES.

ONE OF THESE HYBRID TACTICS IS *HYBRIMEDIA*, THAT IS, A NEW MEDIUM ORIGINATED FROM THE HYBRIDIZATION OF OTHER ORIGINAL MEDIA, SUCH AS CO-PRESENCE MEDIA, CLASSICAL MASS MEDIA AND DIGITAL MEDIA.

THE SOCIAL EFFECTS OF ONE OF THESE MEDIA CAN'T BE UNDERSTOOD WITHOUT THE CONTRIBUTION AND FUSION OF THE OTHER MEDIA, AS IT IS TESTIFIED WITHIN COUNTER-AUSTERITY SOCIAL MOVEMENTS.

3RD CONCLUSION
(SEE RELATED QUESTION 3 AND HYPOTHESIS 3 AT PAGES 6 AND 21)

SOCIAL AND POLITICAL PARTICIPATION ARENAS WITHIN *SOCIAL NETWORKS*, IN PARTICULAR THOSE FIGHTING FOR *COUNTER-AUSTERITY*, CAN'T BE REDUCED TO DIGITAL SOCIAL NETWORKS LIKE FACEBOOK, TWITTER, YOU TUBE, INSTAGRAM, ETC.

THESE CONSTITUTE JUST THE TOP OF THE ICEBERG.

WITHIN CONTEMPORARY SOCIETIES, WE TESTIFY PUBLIC PARTICIPATION PROCESSES BASED ON SINGULAR *ARTICULATIONS AMONG* 3 MAJOR STRATEGIC PILLARS, CORRESPONDING TO *3 CENTRAL NETWORK TYPES*:

1. *PRE-CAPITALIST FACE-TO-FACE NETWORKS*, THAT FEED PROCESSES OF *IDENTITY* AND *DIFFERENCE*, ACTIVATED BY SEVERAL SOCIAL AGENTS AT THEIR LOCALIZED EVERYDAY LIFE.

2. *WEB 2.0 SOCIAL NETWORKS* (FACEBOOK AND THE LIKE) WHERE RAW *INFORMATION*, SOME OPINIONS AND SYNTHETIC ANALYSIS, ARE SHARED.

3. *SOCIAL SEMANTIC NETWORKS* (WEB 3.0), THAT IS, INTERNET SITES WHERE INFORMATION IS TRANSFORMED IN *KNOWLEDGE*, THROUGH THE DEFINITION, INTERPRETATION AND EXPLANATION OF SOCIAL AND POLITICAL PROCESSES, LIKE *COUNTER-AUSTERITY*.

4TH CONCLUSION

EXPERIMENTAL BOOKS DO ENHANCE KNOWLEDGE TRANSFER AND SHARING, AND DEVELOP DIVERSE LITERACY MODES. IN FACT:

1. EXPERIMENTAL BOOKS LIKE *SOCIOLOGICAL COMICS* ARE DIFUSED PUBLICALLY AT DIGITAL LIBRARIES AND SOLD AT DIGITAL BOOKSELLERS AT A LOW PRICE; THEIR PDFS, ABSTRACTS AND TEXT EXTRACTS ARE AVAILABLE IN *OPEN ACCESS AT UNIVERSITIES REPOSITORIES*.

2. THEY DIFFUSE *SOCIAL AND SOCIOLOGICAL STORIES / ACCOUNTS*.

3. THEY DISSEMINATE *SOCIAL AND SOCIOLOGICAL ONTOLOGIES*, THAT IS, INSTRUMENTS THAT ORGANIZE AND DIFFUSE SOCIAL AND SCIENTIFIC CONCEPTS FOR BETTER UNDERSTANDING SOCIAL RELATIONS AND PROCESSES.

4. BIBLIOGRAPHY

ANDRADE, PEDRO (2011).
SEMANTIC-LOGIC SOCIOLOGY OF
WEB 2.0 / WEB 3.0 AT RESEARCH SOCIETY:
EVERYDAY MEANINGS AND DISCOURSES
WITHIN BLOGS, WIKIS, VIRTUAL WORLDS /
MUSEUMS AND SOCIAL SEMANTIC LOGIC
NETWORKS. CALEIDOSCÓPIO
PUBLISHING HOUSE.

ANDRADE, PEDRO; BARROS, JOSÉ;
MARQUES, CARLOS (EDS.),
MILES, MALCOLM ET AL (2010).
PUBLIC ART AND CITIZENSHIP:
NEW READINGS ON THE CREATIVE CITY.
CALEIDOSCÓPIO PUBLISHING HOUSE.
(1ST EDITION SOLD OUT:
A 2ND EDITION IS PREVIEWED).

ANDRADE, PEDRO (1997).
JOURNAL ATALAIA. 3. PP. 197-201.

GIUGNI, MARCO; GRASSO, MARIA
(2015). AUSTERITY AND PROTEST:
POPULAR CONTENTION IN TIMES OF
ECONOMIC CRISIS. ASHGATE PUB.

HAIVE, MAX; KHASNABLISH, ALEX
(2014). THE RADICAL IMAGINATION:
SOCIAL MOVEMENT RESEARCH IN THE
AGE OF AUSTERITY. ZED BOOKS.

MARTINS, MOISÉS (2015).
MEDIA DIGITAIS E LUSOFONIA.
IN M. MARTINS (ED.),
LUSOFONIA E INTERCULTURALIDADE:
PROMESSA E TRAVERSIA (P.28).
V.N. FAMALICÃO: HUMUS.

MENDOZA, KERRY-ANNE (2014). AUSTERITY: THE DEMOLITION OF THE WELFARE STATE AND THE RISE OF THE ZOMBIE ECONOMY. NEW INTERNATIONALIST.

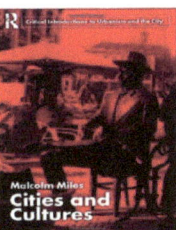

MILES, MALCOLM (2007). CITIES AND CULTURES. ROUTLEDGE.

NEGRA, DIANE; TASKER, YVONNE (EDS.) (2014). GENDERING THE RECESSION: MEDIA AND CULTURE IN AN AGE OF AUSTERITY. DUKE UNIVERSITY PRESS BOOKS.

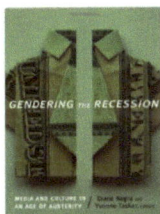

QUE SE LIXE A TROIKA. (2014). [SOCIAL MOVEMENT SITE], RETRIEVED 2013-14, FROM HTTPS://PT-WIKIPEDIA.ORG/WIKI/QUE_SE_LIXE_A_TROIKA!_QUEREMOS_AS_NOSSAS_VIDAS!

5. SOCIAL SOCIOLOGICAL ONTOLOGY

SOCIAL/SOCIOLOGICAL ACCOUNT 11:

THIS ONTOLOGY INCLUDES OLD AND NOVEL CONCEPTS WITHIN A SORT OF 'CONCEPTS NOVEL'.

RECALL THAT A SOCIAL/SOCIOLOGICAL ONTOLOGY MEANS A COLLECTION OF SOCIOLOGICAL MEANINGS ARTICULATED WITH A SOCIAL ARENA, AS IN EACH TERM IN THIS PAGE (SEE ALSO PAGE 5).

'WRITTEN COMICS'

THIS MEANS COMICS INCLUDING NO IMAGES BUT JUST WORDS, LIKE THIS PAGE. THE ORIGINAL PORTUGUESE TERM IS 'BANDA ESCRITA', IN OPPOSITION TO 'BANDA DESENHADA', WHICH LITERALLY MEANS 'DRAWN STRIP'. 'BANDA DESENHADA' IS THE TRANSLATION OF REGULAR 'COMICS' INCLUDING DRAWN IMAGES AND TEXT BALLOONS/LABELS.

AUSTERITOCRACY

AN ECONOMIC, POLITICAL AND CULTURAL PERVERSION OF DEMOCRACY, A PROCESS WHERE HEGEMONIC AND SOMEHOW DICTATORIAL RULES ARE DEMOCRATLY DISSEMINATED FROM A CENTRAL COUNTRY OR A POLITICAL / BUROCRATIC AXIS TO ARTIFICIALLY IMPOVERSHED NATIONS WITHIN WIDE POLITICAL WEBS

URBAN CRITICAL ENCOUNTER

DEFINED AS AN ENCOUNTER IN THE CITY WITH A COLLECTIVE PURPOSE, THAT MAY CONSTITUTE A STRONG PILLAR FOR PARTICIPATION IN THE TRANSFORMATION OF LIFE EVENTS.

EXS: 'MARÉS' OR AN ENCOUNTER FOR READING CRITICAL POETRY.

'MARÉ' ('TIDE')

A CRITICAL AND INNOVATIVE SOCIAL MOVEMENT STRATEGY THAT PARTIALLY DESLIGITIMATES PARTIES AND ENCOURAGES POLITICAL PARTICIPATION OF CITIZENS FROM ALL ORIGINS, WITHIN HUGE CROWDS TO PRODUCE GLOBAL POLITICAL EVENTS.

EVERYDAY GOVERNANCE

A DAILY PARTICIPATION OF CITIZENS TO CRITICIZE ALL FORMS OF EXPLOITATION AND INEQUALITIES, AND FIGHT FOR A DIGNIFIED SOCIAL LIFE.

QUALITATIVE DEMOCRACY

A DEMOCRACY WHERE CITIZENS PREFER LIFE QUALITY AND EVERYDAY GOVERNANCE INSTEAD OF AN ARTIFICIAL QUANTITY OF PERIODICAL VOTES FOR CHOOSING POLITICAL REPRESENTANTIVES.

DIGNIFIED SOCIAL LIFE

THE CONQUEST OF A DIGNIFIED SOCIAL LIFE (CLASS EQUALITY, SEXUAL TOLERANCE, HEALTH, NON-RACISM, FREEDOM, EVERYDAY GOVERNANCE, HUMAN RIGHTS, EDUCATION, CULTURE, CREATIVITY, ETC.) IS ONE OF THE CENTRAL AIMS OF RECENT SOCIAL MOVEMENTS, LIKE THE 'MARÉS'.

LOCAL PUBLIC OPINION

A MODE OF OPINION EXPRESSED BY LOCAL ENTITIES, LIKE COMMUNITIES, ASSOCIATIONS, COLLECTIVES, ETC., ON THEIR SPECIFIC PROBLEMS CONNECTED WITH GLOBAL ISSUES.

SOCIOLOGICAL COMICS

A METHOD FOR DISCUSSING SOCIAL QUESTIONS, USING SOCIAL STORIES AND SOCIOLOGICAL ACCOUNTS, TOLD THROUGH TEXT AND IMAGES WITHIN COMIC FRAMES

DIGITAL PUBLIC SPHERE

PRE-DIGITAL OR DIGITAL SOCIAL NETWORKS ARE SPACES/SCAPES WHERE CITIZENS MEET ONE ANOTHER FOR SOCIAL ENCOUNTERS AND INTERACTION. DIGITAL PUBLIC SPHERE IS A CYBERSPACE AND CYBERTIME TERRITORY WHERE DISCUSSIONS OCCUR, E.G. WITHIN DIGITAL SOCIAL NETWORKS.

HISTORY / STORY

SOCIAL RUPTURES AND HISTORICAL TRANSFORMATION MAY BE VEHICULATED THROUGH SOCIAL STORIES AND SOCIOLOGICAL ACCOUNTS, WHICH INCLUDE SOCIAL PLOTS ARTICULATED WITH POLITICAL, CULTURAL AND ETHICAL ACTION.

SOCIAL ACCOUNT / PLOT

A COLLECTION OR FUSION OF STORIES, COMMENTS, OPINIONS, CRITIQUES, COMMON IDEAS AND EMOTIONS, PRODUCED BY COMMON SOCIAL AGENTS, TO ENGENDER ECONOMIC, POLITICAL, ETHICAL AND AESTHETICAL MEANINGS.

SOCIOLOGICAL ACCOUNT / PLOT

A COMPLEMENTARY INTERPRETATION OF SOCIAL PLOTS, PRODUCED WITH SCIENTIFIC AND ETHICAL OBJECTIVES.

SOCIAL/ SOCIOLOGIST CITIZENS

COMMON CITIZENS AIMING TO PARTICIPATE MORE AND BETTER IN SOCIAL LIFE DEBATES, BY TRANSFORMING INFORMATION INTO KNOWLEDGE, THUS SOMETIMES BECOMING 'LAY SCIENTISTS', OR 'LAY SOCIOLOGISTS'.

WEB 2.0 OR SOCIAL WEB

DIGITAL SOCIAL NETWORKS WHERE USERS READ AND WRITE INFORMATION.

THEY CONSTITUTE A POWERFUL INSTRUMENT OF POLITICAL, CULTURAL AND ETHICAL ACTION.

WEB 3.0 OR SOCIAL SEMANTIC WEB

DIGITAL SOCIAL NETWORKS WHERE CRITICAL USERS TRANSFORM INFORMATION INTO KNOWLEDGE, BY DISCUSSING THE MORE PROFOUND MEANING AND ETHICS OF THEIR ACTIONS AND IDEAS.

6. INDEX